*Cash Making...*

## Web optimization Strategies - Part One

Presentation

The primary objective of any website improvement system is to get your site pages listed. However, even before that can occur, you need to get the internet searcher crawlers to visit your site.

Contingent upon the web index or catalog and the general conditions (how you welcome and request crawlers), that first visit could require days, weeks, or even months.

And keeping in mind that the facts demonstrate that the underlying crawler visits can be fairly unusual (or take quite a while in coming) when the ice is broken, future visits can be controlled somewhat...

Essentially, the more every now and again you update your pages, the more oftentimes the crawlers will appear on your site doorstep.

Obviously, that is just a large portion of the fight. The other half is getting the web crawlers and catalogs to really record your pages.

To do that, you need to begin toward the start. What's more, the start in this specific case is creating and improving pages so that the internet searcher crawlers will be dazzled.

The general hunt measure is straightforward...

All the content substance that internet searcher crawlers assemble is put away and listed. Individuals' direct pursuits are dependent on specific expressions (catchphrases). Whatever substance has the most important with respect to some random watchword will be put in the top places of the list items.

What's more, since the title of the page and the content substance by and large convey the most weight - in any event with respect to what internet searcher crawlers consider generally applicable during their visits - it makes sense that improvement in page rank and additionally indexed lists posting can frequently be ascribed to having individual and explicit catchphrases appropriately consolidated into those two prime zones.

Obviously, if watchwords were the solitary reason for which page rank and position in list items were resolved, advancing site pages would be basically straightforward...

pick a catchphrase > use it in your title and all through your substance >

accomplish high page rank and the top situation in web crawler results

The issue is, there are such countless factors that become an integral factor as well as change consistently, it can appear like accomplishing strong and successful website improvement may never be conceivable.

Luckily, it's not just conceivable, it tends to be generally effortless too. You should simply fulfill the main three prerequisites of basically all significant web crawlers:

- provide quality substance

- update content consistently

- get various highest level sites to connect back to your site

What's more, the web crawlers and catalogs you ought to be attempting to intrigue the most are the main four competitors:

- Google

➢ http://www.google.com

- Yippee

➢ http://www.yahoo.com

- MSN Search

➢ http://search.msn.com

- DMOZ (Open Directory)

> http://dmoz.org

Past that, there are innumerable other web crawlers and registries like AltaVista, Ask Jeeves, and AllTheWeb.

Would it be advisable for you to streamline for those too, or basic level your destinations on the significant players and sidestep all the web crawlers and registries beneath them? Not really. You actually need your pages recorded in however many areas as would be prudent. You just shouldn't attempt to fulfill all of them as to improvement.

Fulfill the main four competitors. At that point, on the off chance that you have the opportunity and desire to expand the extent of your SEO endeavors, do it. If not, don't stress over the hundreds (or even a huge number of) other web crawlers and catalogs that exist.

You're just human. Furthermore, simply meeting the improvement measures of the main four will be testing and adequately enthusiastic.

Obviously, except if you intend to make site improvement your all-consuming purpose, it's not likely you'll put the greater part of your energy in that one single region (in any event, when confined to the main four players). Yet, you do have to contribute a decent measure of value exertion.

What's more, that essentially compares to these two missions...

1. Get your pages filed by significant web crawlers.

2. Improve your page rank and position in list items.

To achieve both of those, you need to deliberately adjust the line between great streamlining strategies and the desire to take things all in all too far.

At the end of the day, you need to verify you do your two missions without venturing over the line into what's ordinarily alluded to as "dark cap" web crawler strategies.

That dull and abhorrent domain would incorporate things like…

Watchword Stuffing - rehashing catchphrases again and again for no coherent or useful explanation

Concealed Content - including catchphrases or text that is a similar tone as the foundation to control internet searcher crawlers

Entryway Pages - not proposed for watchers to see but instead to deceive web crawlers into setting the site into a higher record position

In spite of the fact that these kinds of practices were once viewed as savvy and successful strategies for improvement, they would now be able to bring about having your site restricted from web indexes completely.

As a rule, it's smarter to focus on the most famous and most sensible streamlining strategies. By doing that, you'll not just accomplish the outcomes you're searching for, your endeavors will have dependable outcomes.

Also, when you consider how much work is engaged with getting any site to the highest point of internet searcher rank and position, it merits whatever exertion it takes to take care of business the first run through.

Web crawler Strategy Basics

Generally, there are three fundamental things you'll have to do to achieve legitimate and successful site design improvement.

- compile watchword records

- publish watchword rich substance

- establish a valuable connection methodology

Normally, having programming that can assist you with getting those four things done rapidly and proficiently would be an extraordinary resource. Thus, notwithstanding investigating every one of these territories, we'll incorporate the best programming programs for making each errand simpler to perform.

Catchphrases

The center of any SEO system is fabricated essentially around the gathering of catchphrases you decide to target.

The primary thing to address is to choose which gatherings of catchphrases you'll be using. In many cases, those gatherings will be either straightforwardly or by implication identified with the point or specialty that your site is (or will be) related to.

Whenever you've set up the individual gatherings of watchwords you need to target, you can start to incorporate an exhaustive rundown of high-level expressions that have every one of the accompanying qualities:

- are looked for by a huge number of watchers every single month

- have practically zero rivalries related to it

The more individuals who look for the term joined with minimal measure of rivalry related to it, the more important the watchword will be as to acquiring programmed internet searcher traffic.

Past that, you'll need to arrange arrangements for optional catchphrases. These would even now be significant, however not to the degree that the primary high-level rundown would be.

The primary preferred position of lower-level catchphrases is the way that you don't need to work very as difficult to get complete web crawler acknowledgment. Furthermore, since you'll naturally get a genuinely fair outcomes position, you'll likewise get extra focused on watcher traffic.

To compensate for the absence of value in the watchword itself (as a rule that compares to fewer inquiries being led each month and accordingly less rivalry), you need to work with a lot bigger amount of lower-level catchphrases.

Fundamentally, the outcomes will be similar on a par with what you experience through high-level catchphrases. It will simply take more catchphrases to accomplish those equivalent outcomes.

Obviously, fortunately, there are programming programs that can altogether chop down the measure of time it takes to acquire content - regardless of the number of watchwords you choose to target (see the following portion on Quality Content).

There are a few manners by which you can assemble watchword records. One of the snappiest and least demanding techniques is to utilize the free online proposal device that is given by Overture at http://inventory.overture.com/d/searchinventory/recommendation/.

In spite of the fact that it will give you an obvious sign of the number of searches that have been performed on some random theme during the earlier month, it's to some degree no frills. Additionally, it is extremely unlikely to handily move results from their website page to your autonomously incorporated watchword list.

At the point when you reorder the Overture results, you additionally get the occasions every catchphrase has been looked at. While that may be useful for research purposes, you'll need to physically eliminate that piece of the information to end up with a document that solitary records watchwords.

Wordtracker at http://www.wordtracker.com, then again, does indeed permit you to save your outcomes with only the catchphrases recorded.

You'll need to pay to utilize their online assistance, however, it's certainly justified regardless of the cost. It's profoundly viable and offers the most top to bottom and exact ability concerning genuine pursuits that individuals perform.

Despite the fact that there are various ways you can lead research utilizing Wordtracker, they will all rotate around the capacity to accumulate watchword records which depend on the gatherings of catchphrases you initially settled.

When you know precisely which catchphrases you'll be focusing on, you can start to actualize content that will be related to every one of those expressions.

Quality Content

There are various reasons why "Quality written substance makes all the difference".

From a watcher's point of view, content welcomes them to visit your site as well as urges them to return consistently.

It's a generally straightforward condition:

They're searching for significant data. Offer it to them.

From a web crawler point of view, content is one of the essential factors in deciding exactly how much weight or significance ought to be given to any site page.

Lamentably, this one isn't exactly as basic a condition.

Internet searcher crawlers assemble and list content. Sort out some way to make the place your substance higher on the outcomes stepping stool than some other site.

Obviously, to become King, content should be of impressive quality. To remain, King, content should be refreshed on a genuinely normal premise.

Also, the way that you likewise need to add content (new pages) consistently. If not, whatever ground you at first addition will essentially disappear. Thus will whatever search position or rank you've accomplished.

Normally, you can physically add content by composing everything yourself. Yet, that by itself would be very tedious. Particularly when you consider all the other website admin errands that require your consideration.

So we should discuss mechanizing the assignment all things being equal.

Perhaps the best technique for acquiring quality substance is to incorporate watchword rich articles on your site. What's more, instead of setting aside the effort to keep in touch with them yourself, you can just look for aggregate articles that others have composed.

Obviously, doing that can likewise gobble up a lot of time. To limit the errand - just as upgrade the outcomes - you can basically utilize the accompanying programming program.

- Article Equalizer

> http://www.articleequalizer.com

This permits you to gather up to 1,000 articles with simply the snap of a catch. Also, you can do it dependent on a particular subject or watchword.

Utilize the articles to add quality substance to your current sites or use them to assembled completely new specialty locales. In any case, this is one of the quickest and most effective strategies for social event quality substance.

RSS channels are one more predominant strategy. For acquiring content as well as keeping it new and refreshed also.

Contingent upon what feed or feeds you end up picking, the substance can be as straightforward as a rundown of theme-related connections or as complete as a full-scale, full-page article. What's more, obviously, there's beginning and end in the middle.

The most widely recognized decision for RSS channels is the ones that show a rundown of theme-related URL with a concise depiction underneath everyone. The explanation this sort of feed is most well known is the way that the short depiction permits more potential for focusing on explicit catchphrases.

For instance, if the subject of your site is golf and you need one of your pages to be upgraded for the watchword "golf swing", you would need any substance to incorporate that specific search query.

It's the same as upgrading some other substance on your site. You have a particular catchphrase and you need that expression to be remembered for a particular that it will convey critical load with the web index crawlers.

On the off chance that you can't achieve that, you're only shooting in obscurity, expecting to acquire focused on watcher traffic without really focusing on it.

The objective is to add content that is intended for explicit watchwords. Also, RSS channels are the same as some other substances. On the off chance that it does exclude the catchphrases, you'll simply get web crawler kudos for having nonexclusive point related substance.

Obviously, what you truly need - and need - is to acquire rank and posting profit by whatever substance is added. That is the entire reason... to acquire enough web crawler acknowledgment which thusly gains you focused on watcher traffic.

That being the situation, a definitive programming project would be one that could naturally put RSS channels on your pages while simultaneously do it dependent on explicit watchwords.

Luckily, there is such a program. Furthermore, it's the best programming accessible...

- RSS Equalizer

> http://www.rssequalizer.com

What you accomplish by utilizing RSS Equalizer is a moment topic-based substance, the sort that web indexes like Google are searching for. Furthermore, in light of the fact that the substance changes every single day, you can depend on getting more successive visits from web index crawlers.

So a definitive outcome is exactly the thing you're wanting to acquire... quicker ordering, better pursuit position, and higher page rank.

Connecting Strategies

Picking the correct watchwords and distributing quality catchphrase rich substance puts you around 66% of the route toward ideal web crawler acknowledgment. The other third is basically exclusively dependent on ubiquity.

In the event that we were discussing ubiquity in reality, it would presumably incorporate straightforward things like who has cast a ballot King and Queen of the secondary school prom, or who had the most date alternatives on a Saturday night, or which kin stood out enough to be noticed from Mom or Dad.

In the realm of web crawlers, fame takes on entire diverse importance. What's more, in many occurrences, it comes down to this... the site with the most quality connections highlighting it wins the challenge.

Connection notoriety.

That is the game. Also, a definitive objective is to get innumerable "significant" sites (those that have a subject or theme that is like yours) to give connections back to you. Obviously, when we're discussing significance, we're alluding to how significant web indexes see them.

Frequently, that likens to high page rank and the top situation in query items. The higher up the evolved way of life a site turns out to be, the more remarkable any connection they give back to you is seen.

To get the most blast out of the connection ubiquity measure, it's ideal on the off chance that you really search out significant sites. Besides those you may as of now have as a primary concern, direct inquiries dependent on the catchphrases you're generally keen on acquiring internet searcher acknowledgment for.

Normally, somebody who's in direct rivalry with you wouldn't consider giving you a connection back. So what you've truly searched for are famous sites that have substance or items that are either free to yours or are in a roundabout way.

For instance, suppose your theme and watchword depends on methods of idealizing your golf swing. Great connection back decisions would be sites with the accompanying topics or items:

- information about greens or golf competitions

- golf hardware or attire

- golf educators or classes

On the off chance that the point is identified with yours and the site that is giving the connection back conveys a decent arrangement of weight with significant web crawlers, the estimation of your own site will consequently be raised.

With regards to the real connection that these significant and significant sites put on their pages.

Continuously empower the utilization of text interfaces instead of simply a URL. For instance, rather than essentially showing http://www.adwordanalyzer.com as the connection back to your site, you need something more significant and catchphrase rich. What's more, obviously, internet searchers amicable.

In the event that one of your catchphrases is "directed traffic", for instance, the connection may peruse as follows:

Drive focused on traffic to your site with Adword Analyzer

That not just gives you kudos for the watchword, it empowers the web index crawler to see your site as having more worth.

In the event that you have a different page on your site where you request connect backs, it's consistently a smart thought to show at least one connection text prospects. That way, you'll get kudos for the catchphrases you, at the end of the day, have decided to target.

You ought to likewise give the HTML code to put your connection on different sites. Fundamentally, make it as simple as feasible for another person to add you to their pages.

You ought to likewise indicate where you require a connection back to be set. Preferably, you would need your connection situated on either a landing page or a single tick away from the landing page. In any event, your connection ought to be found where it will be seen as significant by the web index crawlers.

Covered four or five levels profound on some dark page that probably won't be listed is totally useless. The general purpose of getting join backs is to acquire significance with the web crawlers.

So the main concern is:

The more control you have over the connections that others put on their sites, the more web index esteem you'll encounter.

It requires some investment and exertion to urge high-positioning sites to interface back to you. Verify you put whatever extra exertion is essential to acquire the most ideal connection too.

What's more, the standards for the most ideal connection is this:

- It incorporates catchphrase rich content.

- It begins from a significant and high-positioning site.

- It's put in what might be viewed as a significant area.

Anything short of that and you're bargaining the entire connection back cycle.

Continuously remember that in this specific case, the quality will consistently prevail upon the amount. Truly, you need an immense number of connections pointing back to your site. However, given a decision, you're greatly improved with fewer connections from significant sites than incalculable connections from destinations that don't convey a lot of weight with web indexes.

What To Do:

Following is a short outline of what every one of the significant web indexes and catalogs is searching for concerning advancement and worth.

- Google

Doesn't utilize meta portrayal and catchphrase labels. High score for the general weight and nearness of watchwords, < h > labels, and strong content. Prizes quality substance, anyplace between 50 to 600 words.

The substance ought to remember watchwords for text and connections. Likes to see watchwords in the page title (using 90 characters or less) and conveyed reliably all through the site. Particularly esteems interface notoriety, topics, and catchphrases in URL and connection text. The utilization of unreasonable catchphrases, shrouding, and connect ranches is seen as SE spamming.

- Yahoo

No significant significance except for the portrayal and catchphrases filled in assume a job. Won't list anything related to SE spam. Slow stacking pages risk being prohibited. The page title has some importance and ought to be compact. Preferences webpage notoriety and needs to see a topic all through the site.

- MSN

Supports meta depiction and watchword labels. Doesn't list anything related to SE spam. Edges should utilize the <no frames> tag to get filed. Considers the page title significant and needs it to contain catchphrases. Needs to see an appropriate catchphrase recurrence. Connection prominence conveys a decent arrangement of the weight. Likes to see a topic conveyed all through the whole site.

- DMOZ

Likes to see succinct and precise portrayals and watchwords. Slow stacking pages can be punished. The page title has some essentialness and ought to be filled in. Catchphrase recurrence isn't calculated. Connection ubiquity isn't significant. Particularly prefers to see precise and proper classification decisions.

What Not To Do:

After the entirety of your diligent effort getting your pages advanced, the exact opposite thing you need is to accomplish something that would keep your site from getting recorded. Or then again more terrible, have it boycotted via web indexes by and large.

At the highest point of the "don't do" list is the utilization of imperceptible content (the content is a similar tone as the foundation ).

Practically every internet searcher is shrewd to this training and will as of now boycotting any site discovered to utilize it.

Here is a brisk summary of all the other things you ought to never do:

- Try not to rehash watchwords unnecessarily.

- Try not to put unimportant watchwords in the title and meta labels.

- Try not to utilize interface ranches.

- Try not to submit to the wrong classes in inquiry catalogs.

- Try not to submit too many website pages in a single day.

- Try not to distribute indistinguishable pages.

- Try not to utilize meta revive labels

Regardless of how great your site is - regardless of how significant the substance it contains or how lawfully improved it very well may be - on the off chance that you utilize any of the things explained above, you risk being boycotted, marked as a web crawler spammer.

In spite of the fact that it fluctuates starting with one web index then onto the next, spamming can incorporate at least one of the accompanying:

- insignificant page titles and meta portrayal and watchwords labels; reiteration of catchphrases; covered up or tiny content; submitting site pages more than once in a 24-hour range; reflect destinations that highlight distinctive URL addresses; utilizing meta invigorate labels

- With regards to catalogs, for example, DMOZ (which have human editors), spamming by and large likens to one of these three practices:

- the conscious decision of a wrong class inside the index; promoting language; capitalization of letters

- It's not hard to avoid dark cap an area. In any case, it's absolutely hard to recuperate from having utilized those kinds of methods. That is, expecting you can recuperate by any means.

Simply focus on the guidelines set up via web crawlers and registries. Furthermore, since Google is the player you'll most need to fulfill, it's significant that you read and re-read their website admin rules which are distributed at http://www.google.com/website admins/consistently.

Defy the norms and you'll generally be battling to acquire an advantage from all the significant web crawlers. Adhere to the guidelines and you'll set up website pages that won't just be around quite a while, they'll generally be in dispute for top indexed lists position.

Agenda

Catchphrases

- ·Start by building up gatherings of catchphrases that are identified with your picked subjects or territories of interest.

- ·The best catchphrases are ones that are looked for by a huge number of watchers every single month however have little rivalry related to them.

- ·Because optional watchwords are related to fewer pursuits and less rivalry, you'll need to actualize a greater amount of them to accomplish the most extreme advantage.

- ·Keywords ought to be remembered for the title, in < h > labels, and all through the general substance.

- ·Wordtracker is a complete and top to bottom online assistance for ordering exact and powerful catchphrase records.

- ·Don't rehash catchphrases exorbitantly.

- ·Don't utilize improper watchwords in the page title and portrayal.

Quality Content

- ·From a watcher's viewpoint, content welcomes them to visit your site as well as urges them to return consistently.

- ·From a web crawler point of view, content is one of the essential factors in deciding exactly how much weight or significance ought to be given to any page.

- ·You need to add a new substance consistently.

- ·You need content that is refreshed habitually.

- ·Use Article Equalizer ( http://www.articleequalizer.com ) to effectively and rapidly collect and distribute the catchphrase rich substance.

- ·Use RSS Equalizer ( http://www.rssequalizer.com ) to put catchphrase related RSS channels on explicit and individual pages.

Connecting Strategy

- ·The objective is to get endless "significant" sites to give connections back to you.

- ·The higher up the natural way of life a site turns out to be, the more impressive any connection they give back to you is seen.

- ·Actively search out significant sites that have comparative or related topics, items, or data.

- ·Encourage interface backs to incorporate important and watchword rich content as opposed to just a URL address.

- ·The best connections start from high-positioning sites, are set in significant page areas, and incorporate catchphrase rich content.

- ·Pay thoughtfulness regarding the standards set out via web crawlers and catalogs, particularly the website admin rules distributed by Google.

- ·Follow the principles and rules set out via web indexes and registries.

Assets

- Wordtracker

- http://www.wordtracker.com

- One Way SEO Links

- http://www.onewayseolinks.com

- Backlinks Ninja

- http://www.backlinksninja.com

- Suggestion Tool

- http://inventory.overture.com/d/searchinventory/proposal/

- Article Equalizer

- http://www.articleequalizer.com

- RSS Equalizer

  ➢ http://www.articleequalizer.com

- Sitemap Equalizer

  ➢ http://www.sitemapequalizer.com

- Google

  ➢ http://www.google.com/addurl/

  ➢ http://www.google.com/website admins

  ➢ http://www.google.com/website admins/sitemaps/

- Hurray

- http://www.yahoo/information/recommend/

- MSN

- http://beta.search.msn.co.uk/docs/submit.aspx

- DMOZ

- http://dmoz.org/add.html

- AltaVista

- http://www.altavista.com

- Ask Jeeves

- http://www.askjeeves.com

- AllTheWeb

> http://www.alltheweb.com

Cash Making…

Web optimization Strategies - Part Two

Presentation

There's for sure. Streamlining pages to fulfill web crawlers can be a monotonous and requesting task. Initially, however all through the term of any site being live on the web.

Essentially, your site improvement never closes.

You take a stab at high page rank. That can mean a genuine score like the one Google allocates to singular pages or only a reasonable rating that gives your site more web index acknowledgment and height than different destinations in your general vicinity of interest.

In any case, the objective is to make your site more well known, more noticeable, more significant than all the opposition.

You probably won't arrive at the highest point of the pile, yet that is the place where you need to point to land anyplace approach the top.

Not that you can't arrive at the extremely top. You can. It's simply a bit much to receive all the rewards - in any event, from a careful internet searcher viewpoint.

Let's be honest. On the off chance that you land in the main three positions (or even on the primary page) of list items, you'll probably catch a similar measure of traffic that the main site appreciates. Possibly more.

Everything relies upon your depiction. Or on the other hand, should we say, the portrayal that a web index shows in your posting - since meta depiction labels are seldom utilized any longer.

On the off chance that your depiction all the more intently coordinates what a watcher is looking for, they'll go to your site first. Notwithstanding what results in the position you end up being in.

What's more, regardless of whether they don't go there first, they'll in all likelihood arrive ultimately. Except if one of the different sites has absolutely and fulfilled their necessities and they don't feel constrained to proceed with their inquiry.

The fact of the matter is, it's not completely about what position you acquire in web crawler results. It's tied in with focusing on a particular watchword (search term) and afterward verifying you get these two things done...

- Your site positions high for that watchword.

- Your site can convey watcher assumption for that watchword.

Conveying the watcher's assumption is genuinely clear.

On the off chance that the inquiry term is "improve golf swing", it's a quite sure thing the watcher is searching for something to improve their golf swing. However long you give data or an item (or both) that can fulfill that need, you're in amazing striking distance.

Covering the main achievement - getting a high position for your site - is significantly more included.

It's not just about fulfilling a particular watcher need. All things being equal, it's tied in with persuading an internet searcher that your site is better with respect than fulfilling a particular watcher need. For instance...

There are more than 2,000,000 site pages related to improving one's golf swing. Some contain data, some contain items. Some contain nothing more important than a short notice of the pursuit term.

In any case, there are a huge number of pages that appear in the list items all out when a watcher types in "improve golf swing" (roughly 50,000 outcomes on the off chance that you put cites around it, which most searchers do exclude).

You should simply jump into that tremendous expanse of list items and some way or another figure out how to canine oar your page past the wide range of various prospects and onto the sandy seashore. Where a couple of highest level pages are right now luxuriating in the sun.

The solitary inquiry is, how would you achieve that? How would you end up before each one of those other website pages?

You start by breaking down every one of those highest level pages. You filter through their source code, their web content, their plan procedures. Whatever it takes to discover precisely the thing they're doing that set them in the top outcomes positions.

And afterward, you do something very similar. Just better. Furthermore, you continue to do it until you arrive at your definitive objective.

That objective may very well be the main position. Or then again perhaps it's getting recorded in the main three. Or on the other hand, possibly you're willing to make do with any situation on the main page of query items.

It doesn't make a difference.

Whatever objective you've set, whatever position you're going for, you level your sights on the highest level site pages and afterward do all that they're doing and the sky is the limit from there.

Obviously, in case you're focusing on a less pursued inquiry term, you won't need to work close to as hard. Furthermore, that is the reason so many smart website admins do precisely that...

They intentionally search out pursuit terms that are significant to their specific specialty, however, don't have almost the measure of rivalry related to them.

That way, basically actualizing the fundamental improvement procedures will frequently guarantee them a top situation in indexed lists for any of those catchphrases.

You need to know which streamlining strategies work for which web indexes or catalogs. They're all extraordinary. They all set their measures for what components are generally significant.

Some put the best accentuation on connection fame. Others place significantly more incentive on the check and thickness of a particular catchphrase on individual pages. Still, others are keener on seeing an essential subject or theme conveyed all through the whole site.

Luckily, on the off chance that you limit your enhancement endeavors to fulfilling the top players - Google, Yahoo, MSN, and Open Directory (DMOZ) - you can cover the main SEO bases all the while.

For instance, although having the catchphrase in your page title probably won't convey a lot of weight with Yahoo, it's a flat out must with regards to fulfilling Google. So put your catchphrase in the title.

Even though DMOZ couldn't care fewer connections highlighting your page from different sites, Google, Yahoo, and MSN do put a lot of significant worth in how "well known" your page is.

And every one of them needs to see a decent measure of value catchphrase rich substance and a strong point or specialty topic all through.

By fusing the entirety of the main improvement procedures - the ones that are singularly seen as generally significant - you'll see that you have naturally fulfilled the top players.

What's more, discussing top players, Google is the one that you need to point the majority of your time and energy toward. Also, to help you in such a manner, most of this specific report contains Google explicit data.

Focus on ascending to the highest point of Google's outcomes and all the other things will normally become all-good. It's simply that straightforward.

# Website optimization Strategy - Google Style

## Google Webmaster Tools

They're free but then not many website admins exploit the instruments that Google has made accessible. Furthermore, that incorporates Google Sitemaps, perhaps the best technique for getting your pages crept and consequently listed (we'll talk about that one top to bottom in the following section).

Recorded underneath you'll discover a portion of the free SEO instruments that you ought to use consistently.

NOTE: In request to utilize any of these instruments, you'll need a unique key. Simply click on "Get a Free Google API Key" or go to http://www.google.com/programming interface and present the structure. The key will at that point be shipped off whatever email address you determine.

- Google Rankings

- http://www.googlerankings.com/index.php

This apparatus permits you to find the position of the indexed list for some random watchword and URL address. You can include each word in turn or numerous watchwords.

You likewise have three options concerning where the hunt will be directed. That gives you the choice of seeing what position is held in at least one of the three significant competitors... Google, Yahoo, and MSN.

The decent thing about this specific instrument - besides the important data it gives - is that reality that it's moderately quick. Not at all like different instruments of this sort that can require a few minutes to finish the hunt and results measure.

- Google SEO Tool

- http://googlerankings.com/ultimate_seo_tool.php

With regards to watchword improvement, this device is a flat out must. There are two stages included which return data about watchword tally, catchphrase thickness, and watchword position.

Stage 1

Dissect Keywords - Gives you a rundown of 1, 2, and 3 word expresses that seem "x" measure of times or more on some random page ("x" is the sum you pick when first rounding out the structure). You additionally get the thickness rate for each word recorded.

It will likewise show the page title, the meta depiction and catchphrases labels, and the main five frequently utilized watchwords.

Stage 2

Make Position Report - Tells you what position the page holds in Google query items for every one of the best five words found in Step 1.

- Googlerankings Position Tracking

- http://googlerankings.com/positiontracking/

This is an incredible method for keeping steady over the entirety of your internet searcher positions. You make a free record and afterward sign in to enter whatever URL locations and catchphrases you need to monitor.

It permits you to check your positioning history, make graphs, or download information to your accounting page application.

- Google AdWords Keyword Tool

- https://adwords.google.com/select/main?cmd=KeywordSandbox

Utilize this proposal instrument to get thoughts for new catchphrases that can help improve your promotion pertinence. Enter at least one watchword and Google will show you coordinating questions and choices. Can be exceptionally useful when running AdWords crusades.

- Google Suggest

  ➤ http://www.google.com/webhp?complete=1&hl=en

When you begin composing in the inquiry question, Google will start to propose comparable hunt terms. It will likewise show you the number of results that exist for every one of those terms. Exceptionally supportive when gathering watchword records or deciding specialty markets.

- Google Sponsored Links

  ➤ http://www.google.com/sponsoredlinks

Direct an inquiry in Google that profits just supported connection results as it were. This is amazingly helpful when you're attempting to locate the legitimate phrasing for your Adwords or need to perceive how your opposition is getting along.

- Search Term Difficulty Checker

➢ http://www.searchguild.com/trouble/

This one doesn't turn out to be straightforwardly from Google however it has such colossal worth, it unquestionably must be incorporated here.

Everything you do is enter your Google API Key and a pursuit term. (If you don't have an API key, you can get one for nothing at http://www.google.com/programming interface.)

The program will restore a score factor that will tell you how troublesome it is to acquire a situation on the principal page of Google indexed lists for the catchphrase (search term) you just questioned. The lower the score, the simpler it will be.

Presently, at whatever point you concoct a watchword you think may have potential, you can discover immediately whether it's even worth contributing any time and exertion. Both from a traffic creating viewpoint and an SEO position.

Google Sitemaps

Everybody thinks about sitemaps. Customarily, it's a different zone where you remember connections to each open page for your site.

Some of the time they incorporate brief portrayals of the various pages and the substance they contain. Now and again they are just a long and to some degree, a conventional rundown of page joins.

A few people make sitemaps with the sole reason for giving their watchers an extensive site page registry.

A few people make sitemaps essentially to make certain the web index crawlers discover every single accessible page on their site.

And afterward came Google Sitemaps…

Like all internet searcher crawlers, GoogleBot is out there with the express reason for social affairs significant information that can be added to its accessible record. The sooner it can get back with new and refreshed data the better. For both Google and the individuals who utilize their web index.

Given that, the Google sitemap administration offers a twofold arrangement.

To start with, it helps GoogleBot's weight of having to continually slither similar places again and again searching for new and refreshed substances.

Presently, with a framework that advises the bot when and where to creep, the outcome is just a lot of time being saved. The time that can be spent substantially more effectively.

Instead of squandering energy on pages that have not been (and may never be) refreshed or changed, the bot can focus on spots that have important and momentum content that can be added to the inquiry information base.

For website admins, Google Sitemaps offers an approach to send a prompt notice when any change or expansion happens inside their sites.

This not just expands the chance of getting pages ordered quicker, it guarantees that GoogleBot can undoubtedly find pages that are accessible and sidestep all pages that aren't intended to be public.

For the sitemap records themselves, there are two unique sorts that you can execute.

The first is your common rundown of individual pages (much the same as some other sitemap would show). The subsequent kind would be utilized as a list, posting various sitemaps (in the occasion you have multiple).

The cutoff is 50,000 URLs for every sitemap with a limit of 1,000 sitemaps.

Google acknowledges plain content forms however gives a higher need for sitemaps that are written in XML design. That is because the XML adaptation incorporates important warning alternatives that can be related to every URL.

Here is a short clarification of every one of those alternatives.

Last Modified <lastmod>

Permits you to determine the specific time and date a page was last changed or refreshed. This ought to adjust to the ISO 8601 arrangement (you can peruse these details at http://www.w3.org/TR/NOTE-datetime). On the off chance that you decide not to incorporate the time, the configuration for the date alone would be YYYY-MM-DD. Walk 9, 2006, for instance, would be shown as <lastmod>2006-03-06</lastmod>.

Change Frequency <changefreq>

Permits you to indicate how regularly a page will change or be refreshed. Legitimate qualities are consistently, hourly, day by day, week by week, month to month, yearly, and never. Know, nonetheless, that the worth is only utilized as a guide and not an order. It's conceivable that any given page can be slithered pretty much oftentimes than the predefined esteem.

Need <priority>

Permits you to determine a number that tells how significant you feel any page is according to the wide range of various pages on your site. Legitimate qualities range from a flat out low of 0.0 to the greatest high of 1.0 (the default need an estimation of a page is 0.5).

Remember that the need you set has no holding on for respect to what in particular web index results position your page accomplishes (assuming any). It just reveals to GoogleBot which page ought to be given the most significance when creeping your site.

## XML Sitemap Example

```xml
<?xml version="1.0" encoding="UTF-8"?>

<urlset xmlns="http://www.google.com/patterns/sitemap/0.84">

<url>

<loc>http://www.example.com/</loc>

<lastmod>2005-01-01</lastmod>

<changefreq>monthly</changefreq>

<priority>0.8</priority>

</url>
```

```xml
<url>
  <loc>http://www.example.com/page1.html</loc>
  <changefreq>weekly</changefreq>
</url>
<url>
  <loc>http://www.example.com/page2.html</loc>
  <lastmod>2004-12-23</lastmod>
  <changefreq>weekly</changefreq>
</url>
```

```xml
<url>
  <loc>http://www.example.com/page3.html</loc>
  <lastmod>2004-12-23T18:00:15+00:00</lastmod>
  <priority>0.3</priority>
</url>
<url>
  <loc>http://www.example.com/page4.html</loc>
  <lastmod>2004-11-23</lastmod>
```

</url>

</urlset>

## Sitemap Index Example

```xml
<?xml version="1.0" encoding="UTF-8"?>

<sitemapindex xmlns="http://www.google.com/blueprints/sitemap/0.84">

<sitemap>

<loc>http://www.example.com/sitemap1.xml.gz</loc>

<lastmod>2004-10-01T18:23:17+00:00</lastmod>
```

</sitemap>

<sitemap>

<loc>http://www.example.com/sitemap2.xml.gz</loc>

<lastmod>2005-01-01</lastmod>

</sitemap>

</sitemapindex>

Notice the extra .gz expansion. To decrease data transfer capacity, you have the alternative of compacting your sitemap documents utilizing gzip. Uncompressed sitemap documents can't surpass ten megabytes.

Normally, if you have a generally little site, dealing with your sitemap won't be troublesome or excessively tedious. Yet, having a program that computerizes the way toward refreshing and conveying the sitemap would in any case be valuable.

You likely don't have one little site. You in all likelihood have (or will have sooner or later) various sites with hundreds if not a great many pages each. What's more, under those conditions, a robotized framework would be a resource.

Sitemap Equalizer ( http://www.sitemapequalizer.com ) is the best program for doing that. Particularly if you need to verify everything has been dealt with precisely and appropriately.

It gives an incredible web insect that will slither your whole webpage in advance, making sure there are no impasses or traps where a web crawler bug can stall out in a circle, incapable to get to the entirety of your pages.

For more data about Google's sitemap administration, look at the accompanying pages of their site...

Google Sitemaps

http://www.google.com/website admins/sitemaps/

Google Sitemaps Overview

http://www.google.com/website admins/sitemaps/docs/en/navigation.html

Google Friendly Design

No data about SEO technique would be finished without referencing how essential plan components can impact ordering and page rank. Furthermore, in this occurrence, what turns out best for Google essentially applies to all web indexes.

The principal thing you need to comprehend is this...

With regards to great improvement, the one in particular that truly matters - the just a single you need to fulfill - is the web index crawler.

Normally, a pleasant clean plan and a legitimate route are critical to your watcher. However, extraordinary site introduction and execution isn't a lot of good on the off chance that it doesn't conform to internet searcher principles or necessities.

In contrast to watchers, who can see your site both outside and in, internet searcher crawlers just will encounter your site from within, by following the source code through and through.

What's more, they're on a particular mission... to find data that will help file any given page. On the off chance that everything is spread out appropriately, the crawler will have no issue finding watchwords that have been purposely and appropriately positioned inside its way.

That permits the crawler to precisely file your page. Which is the thing that you eventually need. Pages that are ordered by the catchphrases will give you the best advantage.

If the plan is confusing (or causes the source code to contain a huge volume of superfluous components), there's a decent possibility the crawler won't ever concoct a reasonable ordering decision. Furthermore, since the crawler is consistently in a rush, it's not going to stay for any extra or broadened period for your benefit.

On the off chance that, then again, the significant data - the watchwords you've cautiously and meticulously picked - are situated in quite a few places and utilized in the appropriate setting, a crawler won't have a touch of troublesomely deciding precisely how that specific page ought to be filed.

Principally, those crawler-accommodating areas incorporate spots like the page title, obviously noticeable and high-situation < h > labels, and the primary sections and additionally sentences of the principle text content.

Should you consider consolidating the most conspicuous and inventive procedures on your site, reconsider? Doing so is never going to intrigue or request a favor from web index crawlers. (It presumably won't intrigue your human guests.)

Following is an essential rundown of what most internet searcher crawlers can't measure (extricate data from)...

·Image text

·Multimedia, (for example, glimmer and web-based video)

·Pages that require login or treats

·PDF documents

·XML

·Java applets

Likewise, most internet searcher crawlers struggle with things like edges and progressively produced content (for instance, URLs that incorporate "?").

On the off chance that the crawlers can't explore your webpage (and recall that, they're exploring through the source code instead of the external components), they can't appropriately list your site.

A more terrible case situation is that they'll leave rashly and never wind up completely ordering your site.

To advance your pages so that you fulfill both human guests and internet searcher crawlers, you need to do the accompanying:

- utilize the best watchwords for your theme or specialty

- place watchwords where they are best and beneficial

- use watchwords in their legitimate setting

include the right measure of watchwords all through all areas

However long you achieve that, you'll have a site that is individuals neighborly, yet internet searcher agreeable also.

Agenda

^^^^^^^^^^^^^^^^^^^^^^^^^^^^^^^^^^^
^^^^^^^^^^^^^^^^^^^^^^^^^^^^^^^^^^^
^^^^^^^^^^^^^^^^^

·The objective is to make your site more famous, more noticeable, more significant than the opposition.

·Although it's not important to arrive at the main query items position, you need to point there to land anyplace approach to the top.

- If your depiction all the more intently coordinates what a watcher is looking for, they'll go to your site first paying little mind to what your outcomes position turns out to be.

- It's not only about the position. It's tied in with focusing on a particular watchword and afterward making certain your site 1) positions high for that catchphrase and 2) can convey what the watcher is looking for.

- In request to rival sites in top outcomes positions, you need to discover what they're doing and afterward do something very similar, just better.

- If you limit your enhancement endeavors to the top web indexes and registries, you can cover the main SEO bases at the same time.

- Take the preferred position of all the free SEO website admin devices that Google and different sites have accessible.

- Use Google Sitemaps to make certain the crawler discovers every single accessible page/

- Use Google Sitemaps to help get your pages filed quicker.

- Submit XML sitemaps so you can exploit the notice alternatives, for example, the date a page was last adjusted and the recurrence you envision a page will be changed or refreshed.

- Indicating need just tells how significant a page is according to the wide range of various pages on your site. It doesn't matter to what position your page will hold in internet searcher results.

- Use Sitemap Equalizer ( http://www.sitemapequalizer.com ) to make and deal with the entirety of your sitemaps.

·Don't plan your site pages for watchers as it were. Plan them to help search crawlers effectively and rapidly find the particular data and catchphrases that you need your page recorded for.

·Crawler amicable areas incorporate the page title, high situation < h > labels, and the primary passages or sentences of the fundamental content substance.

·Most web index crawlers can't separate data from picture text, mixed media, for example, glimmer and web-based video, pages that require a login, PDF records, XML, and Java applets.

·Most web index crawlers struggle with things like edges and progressively produced substance and pages.

To fulfill the two people and crawlers, you need to use the best watchwords, place catchphrases where they are best, use watchwords in their legitimate setting, and incorporate the right measure of catchphrases all through.

Assets

Google Rankings

http://www.googlerankings.com/index.php

Google SEO Tool

http://googlerankings.com/ultimate_seo_tool.php

Googlerankings Position Tracking

http://googlerankings.com/positiontracking/

Google AdWords Keyword Tool

https://adwords.google.com/select/main?cmd=KeywordSandbox

Google Suggest

http://www.google.com/webhp?complete=1&hl=en

Google Sponsored Links

http://www.google.com/sponsoredlinks

Search Term Difficulty Checker

http://www.searchguild.com/trouble/

Google Sitemaps

http://www.google.com/websiteadmins/sitemaps/

Google Sitemaps Overview

http://www.google.com/websiteadmins/sitemaps/docs/en/navigation.html

ISO 8601 Date and Time Formats

http://www.w3.org/TR/NOTE-datetime

Sitemap Equalizer

http://www.sitemapequalizer.com

www.ingramcontent.com/pod-product-compliance
Lightning Source LLC
Chambersburg PA
CBHW070301220526
45465CB00004B/1695